What Can You Do with Rice?

By Cameron Macintosh

What do you think about rice?

I love it because rice can go with so many foods.
You can eat rice with whatever you want.

Shall we find out what you can do with rice?

Rice is easy to cook.

You can boil it, steam it or fry it!

Nan asks me what kind of rice I want today.
I say I want boiled rice!

boiled rice

fried rice

First, Nan washes the rice. Then she puts it in a pot of water, adds a pinch of salt and puts a lid on the pot.

When the rice is cooked,
I make sushi.

I put raw fish on top of wads
of rice.

If you don't want fish, you could
swap it for meat.

Sometimes I want rice balls, so I get a wad of rice and put some cooked fish inside.

Then I squash it all together and put seaweed on the outside.

I also like fried rice with some hot spices.

The yummy smell wafts up to my nose!

Once, I got to visit a place where people grow lots of rice.

I got to wander around the rice fields.
It was amazing!

The rice plants need **lots** of water, so the fields are like a swamp!

When it's time to pick the rice, people squat in the fields and cut the plants.

Since I got back, I want all my meals to have rice!

What kind of rice snack can I have?
I can put some radish on a rice cake with cheese.

I wander into the kitchen to watch Great Gran make a rice meal for lunch.

So, what can you do with rice?

Whatever you want!

CHECKING FOR MEANING

1. What are two of the ways you can cook rice? *(Literal)*
2. What do rice plants need? *(Literal)*
3. Do you think the narrator enjoyed the trip to see where rice plants grow? Why? *(Inferential)*
4. What do you think is the best way to eat rice? *(Evaluative)*

EXTENDING VOCABULARY

sushi	Which country does sushi come from? Do you know any other foods from that country?
wafts	The word *waft* is often used in relation to smells. What does a smell do if it wafts?
squat	Describe what someone is doing if they squat.

MOVING BEYOND THE TEXT

1. Rice is a very versatile food. Tell me about a time that you've eaten rice. Was it spicy? Was it salty? Did you like it?
2. Which food from the text would you like to try? Are there any foods that you do not like?
3. Have you ever helped to cook a meal? How did you help? Did you chop or mix anything?
4. If you could eat one food for every meal, what would it be? Why?

TIME TO WRITE

Write about your favourite food and the best way to eat it.